HURRICANE!

The 1900 Galveston Night of Terror

by Donna Latham

Consultant: Daniel H. Franck, Ph.D.

PUBLISHING COMPANY, INC.

New York, New York

Credits

Cover, Courtesy of Rosenberg Library, Galveston, Texas; Bettmann/Corbis; Jose Luis Pelaez, Inc./Corbis; NASA Johnson Space Center (NASA-JSC); Title Page, Courtesy of Rosenberg Library, Galveston, Texas; 4, Joe Skipper/Reuters/Corbis; 5, Courtesy of Rosenberg Library, Galveston, Texas; 7, Courtesy of Rosenberg Library, Galveston, Texas; 8–9, Courtesy of Rosenberg Library, Galveston, Texas; 10, Steve Stankiewitz; 11, NASA Johnson Space Center (NASA-JSC); 13, Tim Boyles/Getty Images; 14, Bettmann/Corbis; 15, Courtesy of Rosenberg Library, Galveston, Texas; 16, Alan W. Jones/Best Shot Aerial Photo; 17, Courtesy of Rosenberg Library, Galveston, Texas; 18–19, Courtesy of Rosenberg Library, Galveston, Texas; 20, Clara Barton National Historic Site, National Park Service; 21, Courtesy of Rosenberg Library, Galveston, Texas; 22–23, Courtesy of Rosenberg Library, Galveston, Texas; 24, AP Wide World Photos; 25, AP Wide World Photos; 26, Lou Ann Cunningham; 27, AP Wide World Photos.

Original design and production by Dawn Beard Creative, Triesta Hall of Blu-Design, and Octavo Design and Production, Inc.

Library of Congress Cataloging-in-Publication Data

Latham, Donna.
  Hurricane! : the 1900 Galveston night of terror / by Donna Latham ; consultant, Daniel H. Franck.
    p. cm. — (X-treme disasters that changed America)
  Includes bibliographical references and index.
  ISBN 1-59716-071-7 (lib. bdg.)—ISBN 1-59716-108-X (pbk.)
1. Hurricanes—Juvenile literature. 2. Hurricanes—Texas—Galveston—History—20th century—Juvenile literature. I. Title. II. Series: X-treme disasters that changed America.

  QC945.L38 2006
  551.55'2—dc22

                        2005005207

For more information, write to Bearport Publishing Company, Inc., 101 Fifth Avenue, Suite 6R, New York, New York 10003. Printed in the United States of America.

1 2 3 4 5 6 7 8 9 10

Table of Contents

Warning on the Beach

It was early Saturday, September 8, 1900. Dr. Isaac (EYE-zic) Cline was frightened. An enormous storm was coming toward Galveston Island, Texas.

Dr. Cline was chief **meteorologist** for the U.S. Weather Bureau. He had received warnings of a **hurricane**. Dr. Cline hadn't worried since hurricanes were uncommon in Galveston. Now, however, he was alarmed.

▲ Dr. Cline observed storm swells—long, unbroken waves caused by storm winds—like the ones in this photo.

Huge walls of water formed as winds gained power. Giant waves hammered the shore. The high tide sprawled over the land. It was time, Dr. Cline decided, to warn people of disaster. He leapt onto his horse and hurried to the beach.

"Head for the mainland!" he cried.

◀ Dr. Isaac Cline

People were trapped on Galveston Island when the hurricane caused a steamship to crash through the bridges that connected the island to the mainland.

Nature's Fury

The hurricane's wind grew ferocious. Dr. Cline's helpers measured its speed at 100 miles per hour (161 kph). By 3 p.m., the whole island was underwater. Dr. Cline sloshed home through waist-high waters. He urged 50 people to take shelter in his home.

Dr. Cline's **anemometer** was ripped away before the hurricane's strongest winds hit. Today, scientists estimate that the winds reached 140 miles per hour (225 kph).

At 7:30 p.m., from his front door, Dr. Cline watched nature's **fury**. Wind and rain destroyed houses. Trees were ripped from the ground.

"Roofs of houses and timbers were flying through the streets as though they were paper," he wrote.

To leave the house meant certain death. People might be swept away by water. Flying **debris** could kill them.

▲ Moving like a steamroller, the hurricane leveled Galveston, crushing everything in its path.

A City Swept Away

By the next morning, at least 8,000 people were dead. Bodies of people and animals littered the city. Crushed wood and stone were everywhere. In all, 3,636 homes were destroyed. Damage totaled more than $760 million in today's money.

Some taller buildings survived the storm.

The island city had been swept away by the storm and its 16-foot (5-m) waves. Dr. Cline's house had been swallowed in the night.

"Among the lost was my own wife," he wrote. She "never rose above the water after the wreck of the building."

Over 100 years have passed since the Hurricane of 1900. Yet, it remains the worst **natural disaster** in U.S. history.

Galveston had been built over sand. When the hurricane hit, the city's battered buildings crumbled like sand castles.

What Is a Hurricane?

Only storms with certain **features** are called hurricanes. These storms form over warm areas of the oceans. They cover huge areas of water and include pounding rains. Their winds swirl around a calm center, called the eye of the hurricane. The winds blow at speeds of 74 to over 200 miles per hour (119–322 kph).

Hurricane

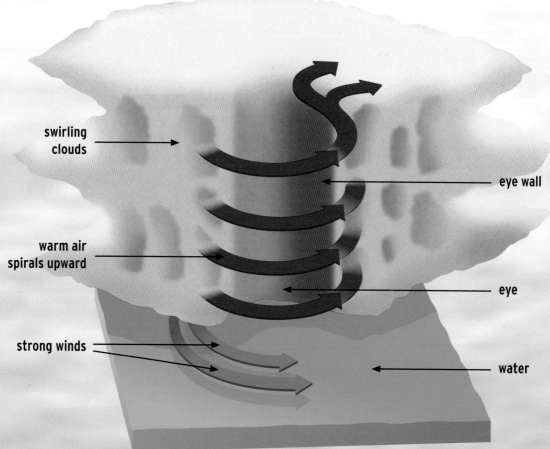

swirling clouds

warm air spirals upward

strong winds

eye wall

eye

water

A hurricane is a storm on the move. Lasting from 3 to 14 days, it can travel at 5 to 20 miles per hour (8–32 kph). It may travel as far as 4,000 miles (6,437 km) before it dies out.

The eye of a hurricane covers a huge area—15 to 20 miles (24–32 km).

Hurricanes usually strike in summer and early fall. Coastal areas and islands are at risk.

Four Hurricanes in Two Months

Around August 27, the Hurricane of 1900 formed in the Atlantic Ocean. On September 4, it crossed Cuba. Before reaching Texas, it gained speed near Key West, Florida.

Even today, the Florida coast remains a hurricane target. During August and September 2004, it suffered four violent hurricanes. Charley struck first, with winds of 180 miles per hour (290 kph).

Florida Hurricanes, 2004

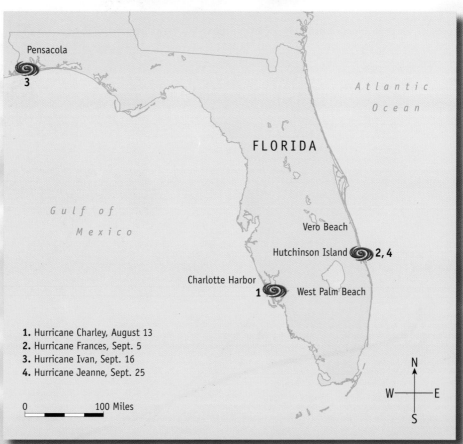

Pensacola
3

Atlantic Ocean

FLORIDA

Gulf of Mexico

Vero Beach

Hutchinson Island 2, 4

Charlotte Harbor
1   West Palm Beach

1. Hurricane Charley, August 13
2. Hurricane Frances, Sept. 5
3. Hurricane Ivan, Sept. 16
4. Hurricane Jeanne, Sept. 25

0 ——— 100 Miles

N
W — E
S

Ten-foot (3-m) waves flooded roads. Power poles were blown down. Wind blasted roofs off hospitals and emergency centers. One girl died when the wind hurled a van into traffic.

After Charley passed, more destruction was soon to come. Over the next six weeks, three other hurricanes struck Florida.

▲ Hurricane Charley
demolished trailer parks.

The 2004 Florida hurricanes claimed over 70 lives. They caused billions of dollars in damage.

The Texas Storms of 1886

It is rare for four hurricanes to hit one state in a year. In 1886, over a century before Florida's 2004 storm season, however, Texas was clobbered four times. The first storm crashed into Sabine, Texas, in June. The tide rose to over nine feet (3 m). Fortunately, no one died.

In 1967, heavy rain and violent winds toppled this boat in Brownsville, Texas.

In August, the second storm flooded Indianola, Texas. Shattered houses covered the coast. Not one home survived. The third storm, in September, hit the same area.

In October, the fourth hurricane slammed Sabine again. This time, 150 people died. Over 100 drowned in a huge **tidal wave**.

◄ Indianola was never rebuilt after the hurricanes of 1886.

Bits of pottery, antique pocket watches, and old hat pins still wash up on Indianola's beaches. They are lonely reminders of the town's past.

Tales of Survival

After the Hurricane of 1900, stories of how people survived swept Galveston. Some people had scrambled onto roofs. Others had hung on to pieces of buildings.

Dr. Cline and his three children drifted through the night atop a wall from their home. Dr. Cline's wife, however, was not so lucky. A month after the storm, her body was found floating on another piece of the house wall.

◀ Bishop's Palace, a beautiful mansion in Galveston, proved a sturdy shelter. The 200 people who ran inside it during the storm survived.

St. Mary's **Orphanage** was one of the first buildings smashed by the storm. Ten nuns and 93 children had lived there. Sadly, only three boys survived. They hung on to an uprooted tree as it rode the waters.

▼ St. Mary's Orphanage before the hurricane

Near the beach, St. Mary's Orphanage was one of the storm's first targets. Almost everyone who lived there was killed.

Heat, Debris, and a Changed Opinion

After the storm, Galveston was still full of danger. **Humidity** and high temperatures caused dead bodies to smell. The terrible odors made people ill. Blowing debris often struck survivors. **Looters** robbed damaged homes and even stole from bodies on the streets.

Clean-up crews tried to make the city safer. However, their jobs grew more difficult when bodies that were buried at sea washed back onto the shore.

▼ Every person in Galveston lost family or property due to the hurricane.

Dr. Cline had once believed that a seawall was not needed in Galveston. The hurricane changed his mind.

The Goal to Rebuild

Soon after the storm, a special group formed. Its members planned to clear away the rubble. They arranged to bury the dead properly.

Red Cross founder Clara Barton brought help to the Galveston survivors.

The people of Galveston would not allow their city to become a ghost town, like Indianola. Galveston had been an important **port** before the hurricane. Being close to the sea had made it a rich, strong city of 37,000 people. Vacationers visited its beaches. After the storm, people vowed to rebuild an even better city.

▼ Galveston before the hurricane

Two Major Changes

Two major changes took place in Galveston after the storm. First, a three-mile-long (5-km) seawall was built between 1902 and 1904. It protects the city from floods.

Second, the entire city's **elevation** was raised to a higher level. Flooding would be less likely on higher ground. Over 2,100 buildings were lifted up. **Dredges** were used to dig up sand. Then, about six feet (2 m) of sand was poured under each building.

During this time, people walked on raised wooden sidewalks. It took eight years to complete the huge project. In all, 500 city blocks were lifted.

▼ New sections were added to the Galveston seawall over the years. The final section was finished in 1962. The present seawall is more than ten miles (16 km) long and about 17 feet (5 m) high.

In 1915, another hurricane slammed Galveston. Due to the safety changes made to the city, only eight lives were lost.

Feeling Safe, Feeling Curious

In 1900, there was no television or Internet. Instead, weather news spread by telephone and telegraph. It traveled through word of mouth. Sailors, for example, had warned of the Galveston hurricane.

Dr. Cline realized too late how **severe** the storm would be. People didn't hurry to leave when he warned them. They felt they would be safe in their homes.

Hurricane **evacuation** routes are now in place for people in coastal areas.

People were also curious. They flocked to the beach to watch the monstrous waves. Children splashed in the rising waters.

Soon, bridges collapsed. Winds ripped trains from their tracks. Telephone and telegraph wires crashed down. People were trapped.

◀ Today, people receive warnings well before hurricanes strike. In 1998, more than 330,000 people evacuated Nags Head, North Carolina, to avoid Hurricane Bonnie.

Storm Tracking

In 1900, information about the weather moved slowly. The U.S. Weather Service in Washington, D.C., had only been started in 1890. **Forecasting** the path of hurricanes, moreover, was a new science. After the Galveston storm of 1900, however, great changes in the way weather is studied took place.

▲ A monument to the Hurricane of 1900 stands near the Galveston seawall.

Dr. Cline wrote textbooks about tropical storms. His work became very important to other scientists.

Today, meteorologists use computers and **satellites** to track storms. They can often warn people of a storm three or four days before it hits. These warnings save lives.

The Hurricane of 1900 changed Dr. Cline. After that September night, he made the study of tropical storms his life's work. He didn't want people to face such a disaster ever again!

▲ Satellite images help meteorologists track hurricanes and give warnings.

Just the Facts

Hurricanes and people have clashed throughout history.

- **The Ancient Maya (A.D. 250–900)**—Hurricanes were common for the Maya Indians of Mexico and Central America. The word *hurricane* probably comes from the name of their storm god, Hurukan.

- **The Treasure Coast (1715)**—Spanish ships toting $300 million in gold and silver set sail from Havana, Cuba. A huge hurricane destroyed the ships. It killed over 1,000 people. The treasure remains at the bottom of the ocean. This area of Florida, including Hutchinson Island, Port Salerno, and Port St. Lucie, is now called the Treasure Coast. In 2004, Florida's hurricanes struck this very area.

- **The Philippines Typhoon (1944)**—A Pacific Ocean hurricane is called a typhoon. During World War II, a typhoon hit the Philippines. Its winds of 125 miles per hour (201 kph) slammed U.S. Admiral William Halsey's fleet. Three warships sank. About 800 sailors died.

The Hurricane of 1900 left the entire city of Galveston in ruins.

- Nearly every family lost at least one person.
- 10,000 survivors were homeless.
- Thousands of freezing survivors needed clothing. The storm had torn clothes from their bodies.
- Bodies of people, dogs, chickens, horses, and cows jammed waters.
- The city was without electric, telephone, or telegraph lines. There was no fresh water or transportation.

Improvements that have made cities in the United States safer since the Galveston hurricane:

- Seawalls protect coasts from storm surges.
- Storm tracking allows warnings to be timely.
- Evacuation plans and routes are in place.

Today, hurricane forecasters rate the damage storms are likely to cause. They use categories from 1 to 5. The Galveston storm was a Category 4.

The Saffir-Simpson Hurricane Scale		
Category	Level	Wind Speed
1	slight	74–95 mph (119–153 kph)
2	moderate	96–110 mph (154–177 kph)
3	strong	111–130 mph (179–209 kph)
4	very strong	131–155 mph (211–249 kph)
5	catastrophic	over 155 mph (over 249 kph)

Source: National Oceanic and Atmospheric Administration

Glossary

anemometer (an-i-MOM-uh-tur)   an instrument used to measure wind speed

debris (duh-BREE)   scattered pieces of houses, buildings, and other objects, left after a storm

dredges (DREJ-iz)   machines used to dig sand or mud

elevation (el-uh-VAY-shun)   an area's height above sea level

evacuation (i-*vak*-yoo-AY-shun)   the removal of people from a dangerous area

features (FEE-churz)   important parts or qualities of something

forecasting (FOR-kast-ing)   saying what you think will happen in the future

fury (FYOO-ree)   wild and dangerous force

humidity (hyoo-MID-uh-tee)   the level of moisture in the air

hurricane (HUR-uh-kane)   a violent storm with very high, swirling winds

looters (LOO-turz)   robbers

meteorologist (mee-tee-ur-OL-oh-jist)   a scientist who studies the weather

natural disaster (NACH-ur-uhl duh-ZASS-tur)   an event caused by nature that results in great loss, hardship, and damage

orphanage (OR-fuh-nij)   a place where orphans (children whose parents are dead) live and are cared for

port (PORT)   a place where ships load or unload

satellites (SAT-uh-lites)   spacecrafts sent into space to send information back to Earth

severe (suh-VEER)   very strong or intense

tidal wave (TIDE-ul WAYV)   a huge, powerful ocean wave moved by strong winds

Bibliography

Heidorn, Keith. "Dr. Isaac M. Cline: Converging Paths: A Man and a Storm." *Weather People and History.* www.islandnet.com/~see/weather/history/icline2. htm (2000).

Hughes, P. "The Great Galveston Hurricane." *Weatherwise* 43, no. 4 (August 1990): 190.

Lutz, Heidi. "The 1900 Storm: Tragedy and Triumph." *Galveston County Daily News.* www.1900storm. com/index.lasso (2004).

NOAA. "Galveston Storm of 1900." *NOAA History: A Science Odyssey.* www.history.noaa.gov/stories_ tales/cline2.html (2004).

Read More

Berger, Melvin, and Gilda Berger. *Hurricanes Have Eyes But Can't See and Other Amazing Facts About Wild Weather.* New York: Scholastic Reference (2004).

Challoner, Jack. *Hurricane & Tornado.* New York: DK Publishing (2004).

Galiano, Dean. *Hurricanes.* New York: Rosen Publishing Group, Inc. (2000).

Simon, Seymour. *Hurricanes.* New York: HarperCollins (2003).

Learn More Online

Visit these Web sites to learn more about the Hurricane of 1900:

www.noaa.gov/galveston1900/

www.1900storm.com/

Index

About the Author

A former school librarian, Donna Latham is a writer
in the Chicago, Illinois, area.